GW00458216

#Christian Straight Talk

Ben Cooper & Simon Pinchbeck

Scripture quotations marked NKJV are from the *New King James Version.* Copyright © 1982 by Thomas Nelson Inc. Used by permission. All rights reserved.

Scripture quotations marked AMPC are taken from the *Amplified® Bible,* Copyright © 1954, 1958, 1962, 1964, 1965, 1987 by The Lockman Foundation. Used by permission.

Scripture quotations marked *NLT* are from the Holy Bible, New Living Translation, copyright 1996. Used by permission of Tyndale House Publishers, Inc., Wheaton, Illinois 60189. All rights reserved

Dedication

This book is dedicated to men that are tired of church, tired of life and are hungry for Jesus Christ.

Acknowledgement

All glory goes to the Father, our fellowship through Jesus Christ the inspiration, and revelation from the Holy Spirit.

> *"I am the Lord that is my name I will not yield my glory to another or my praise to idols"*
> *(Isaiah 42v8)*

Table of Contents

Preach the word; be instant in season, out of season; reprove, rebuke, exhort with all long suffering and doctrine.

For the time will come when they will not endure sound doctrine; but after their own lusts shall they heap to themselves teachers, having itching ears;

And they shall turn away their ears from the truth, and shall be turned unto fables.

But watch thou in all things, endure afflictions, do the work of an evangelist, make full proof of thy ministry.

2 Timothy 4 v 2-5

Introduction

#Christian Straight Talk – The Background story

Ben Cooper and Simon Pinchbeck are the founders of #Christian Straight Talk. They fondly refer to themselves as 2 blokes with a Bible from Kent and Essex looking for Jesus and following Jesus.

They have been meeting regularly since being introduced some 3 years ago. Ben and Simon found that they were 'on the same page' when it came to life, and how by accepting Jesus and following Him, their lives could be radically transformed. They started their Podcast which focuses primarily on following Jesus and addressing real life problems as a result of these meetings. Their weekly Podcasts can be found at #ChristianStraightTalk on Spotify.

Since being introduced to each other around three years ago through a mutual friend, Ben and Simon firmly believe it was God moving and bringing them together for such a time as this. The motivation behind the Podcast was the conversations they regularly had about the word of God.

At the start of the first COVID-19 lockdown, they felt a stirring from God to speak about real life problems - without holding back - bringing into the arena #Christian Straight Talk; scripture always being at the centre of their conversation. They felt God very clearly moving them through the Podcasts as the door opened quickly and easily and it all just came together.

Their aim, primarily, is to introduce men and women to Jesus and to encourage them to experience freedom by letting go of stuff that is holding them back and being who God created them to be.

About Reverend Ben Cooper

Ben came to faith in Jesus as a teenager. He left school a year early after becoming despondent because his dyslexia was not recognised and he started work as a Hod carrier. He completed a 3 year apprenticeship in bricklaying, gaining a City and Guilds qualification; during this time he was in rebellion to God's calling but later, following a 'God Moment', he committed to his calling. He remained in the building trade until his ordination.

2

INTRODUCTION

Ben's passion to preach and teach resulted in him heeding to the call of God when he committed to completing the Church Training Program at Elim Bible College. He was very active in Prison Fellowship and was also appointed to serve as Chaplain to the Mayor for 3 consecutive years.

Reverend Ben Cooper is the Senior Minister at Elim Church Swanley which is a very lively and busy missional church. Ben is passionate about the Word of God and really enjoys his preaching, teaching and pastoral role. He is also Lead Chaplin at a local Hospice where he journeys with people at the most vulnerable time of their life. Ben also sits on the Board of Directors for a local housing association.

Ben enjoys engaging in theological studies and debates and has never allowed his dyslexia to hold him back or detract him from achieving his goals.

Ben is married to Kris who is also very active in the church and their daughter Molly is studying at University.

About Simon Pinchbeck

Simon was a 'Copper' who crossed paths and became a 'Criminal' then changed his direction in life to become a 'Christian'.

After 23 years Simon left London's Met Police upon receiving a `Not Guilty' verdict at Crown Court on a serious assault charge. He then became obsessed with money and succumbed to a life of crime with a group of men that trained at a local gym.

However, after a nasty falling out with these guys, Simon faced prison or death. He had left his wife and family and was at the lowest point of his life.

In 2002, after seeing the difference that Jesus Christ had made in the life of a very violent man, Simon invited Jesus into his own life - and since then has been reunited with his family and continued to let Jesus tell His story, through Simon's life, across the UK and beyond.

Since becoming a Christian in 2002, Simon has been involved with the Alpha Course, and Prison Ministry at Holy Trinity Brompton. He is part of the power lifting evangelistic ministry of Tough Talk, and has been a Regional director with Christian Vision for Men. He was the UK lead of QuestLife, a `Freedom` ministry from Texas.

Simon is currently the lead in a ministry named Bold Encounter, another `Freedom` ministry, and is involved with the Union of Evangelical Churches, 15 churches across London and Essex – helping with their events and their `Men`s Stuff`.

He shares the story of Jesus through his life, across the UK and beyond. Like Ben, he has a real passion to tell people the `Good News` of Jesus Christ, and see men and women `set free` from the stuff that holds them back, from being the people that God made them to be.

Simon has been married to Lynda for over 30yrs. He has two sons, Tom and Jamie, and two grandkids Scarlett who is 6yrs old and George who is four. He supports Arsenal football club, and likes to tell bad jokes!

Why you need this book

The content of this book #Christian Straight Talk is drawn from excerpts of the Podcast that Ben and Simon host. Their Podcasts are now being put into book form, giving the reader an amazing insight into the revelations they received through their conversations. They felt that putting the Podcasts into book form was an extra avenue for the word of God to be used, as the Lord was leading.

This book titled #Christian Straight Talk -Men's Talk, is one of many in the series of #Christian Straight Talk books. It deals specifically with issues which affect men that are rarely spoken about especially in the church.

Over the years, Simon has been an encourager of men running several events and speaking at many others, helping men find their way to the Father through Jesus. God has used him powerfully and he has a wealth of knowledge when it comes to men's issue. Reverend Ben on the other hand has been a minister of the gospel for many years also ministering to many men alongside other members of his congregation and also has a wealth of knowledge and experience.

Joining forces, Ben and Simon have come together through their funny but serious chats to provide hope for the real men out in the world today. Without the strap lines of the church and all the clichés, they bring out real life situations and offer a way forward for men as the Holy Spirt leads them. The goal of this book is to help men move forward daily, "getting to guys that really need Jesus and cutting out all the fluffy stuff" stuff that does not address the real issues men face. In this book, all those **real** issues are addressed and men are encouraged to enjoy the benefits of the covenant of Fatherhood (with God) as they are being made whole.

The conversations are honest, completely open and sometimes brutally truthful; they do not hold back and say it as it is. They discuss what it is like to be a Christian man in the instituted church. They are not into theology and all that stuff –just following Jesus

If you are looking for real talk, genuine talk about men's issues you will find it here. Get ready to be blessed as they share what has been laid in their hearts in an authentic way with snippets of unapologetic British dry humour.

It is their hope that people's lives will be changed and souls saved through the reading of this book.

Father's Arms

Men struggle with their identity. When they meet people, most times, they are questioned about who they are and what they do for a living. Often, they try to fit themselves into these roles. However, identity is not in the church building, or denomination. It is not in what you have, do, or even the size of your congergation. Rather a man's identity should be in the living Christ, whose word is sharper than a two edged sword. Identity should be about identifying oneself as just a son of the living God.

Many men have problems with their earthly fathers but following Jesus will lead them to the Father. The Bible says *"I am the way the truth and the life no one can comes to the father except through me"* John 14:6. Our journey is to follow Jesus to the Father and the Father goes, "my son, my son". Following Jesus by inviting and accepting Him is not the whole story or the full treasure. The treasure is following Jesus to the Father. Once you follow Jesus to the Father and find the love of the Father, it is incredible.

8

It is so emotional and surreal to realise that no matter what we may have done, no matter where we are, God still loves and accepts us. The story of the prodigal son springs to mind here. He was so eager to get his inheritance and get on with his life but his father despite everything was patiently waiting for him to come back home. There is nothing that we can do that will make the Father reject us. No matter what, HE will be there for us to our last breath; He will carry us. The father saw the son coming back even before the son decided to go back. And while the son was worried about what his father was going to say and do, the father's concern was that his son was coming home. He ran out and put the best robe on his son and prepared a feast for him. It is the same with Jesus, there is nothing too big for Jesus to forgive you for "Come home to Jesus, just come home".

Simon's personal story is a real prodigal story. He had reached the point where he was lying in the dirt but the night he reached the church where he said the prayer, the Father said to him "it is time to get out of the dirt; accept my son Jesus and come home".

There is nothing more powerful; the feeling of the Father's arms around you cannot be compared to anything, the peace, the stillness, it is difficult to articulate, trying to explain that feeling is hard. Trying to explain how that feels, to know that no matter what one has done Jesus will forgive them, is tough. Knowing however, that we are washed in His blood and it does not matter if we slip and slide or make mistakes, He is there, just waiting to embrace us is liberating.

Unfortunately, the church does not teach that the arms of the Father are open. It does not teach about the Father's love or the power in the name of Jesus (we don't hear the gospel message being preached about repentance and forgiveness) and what it is to come to the cross and to the Father. But forgiveness is such a big word and a lot of men are looking for just that; forgiveness for the way they think or have lived. Forgiveness is a word very liberally used in Christian circles but repentance is hardly talked about. However, before you get forgiveness there has to be repentance and repentance is not just saying forgive me Father but it is about turning away, making an about-turn, and that is impossible to do without Jesus.

Many people find it difficult to figure out what they are repenting of but according to Ben repenting daily should become a lifestyle. Asking God to forgive you for the little things that happen in your daily life, saying "Lord help me, I got caught up in something today that I should not have", is freeing. When you start to realise that "*All have sinned and fallen short of the glory of God*", you understand that you will never get everything right, no one will... It is impossible. It is only by the grace of God, the power of repentance and scripture being fulfilled that we stand, because none of us is worthy.

Why you need Jesus

We have people in the world who do not know Jesus Christ but they have a sense of what is good or right, but they don't understand what sin is so they say, "I'm a good guy, I give to charity, I cut a few corners on my tax return but I am a decent guy", so why do I need this Jesus you keep talking about. When someone says this, the first answer is that without Jesus they will end up in an eternity that is full of pain and torment; good works do not get one into the Kingdom. Again the church does not preach that good works alone will not lead to eternity. Asking people simple questions like, have you told a lie before? have you stolen anything in life?, e.g. pencils, pens etc. have you ever hated anybody in your life? These questions show that we are all guilty. We are guilty of lying, cheating and even murder because the bible says (if you hate someone in your heart it is like murder.) This

11

is shocking to hear because people will say, 'I live in a beautiful postcode and work in the city and you call me a liar?', but it is a fact. If we can put our hands up to all that stuff then we are on the road to recovery and on the right track because we are standing in the dock, having admitted our guilt and we deserve to be sentenced. But Jesus, who is the judge steps out, comes into the dock puts his arm around us and says "accept me and I will PAY THE PRICE. You are forgiven, the slate is wiped clean".

There is no one like Jesus

There is nowhere else that you can get this kind of love. No matter where you look in every religion, you will not find a saviour that will step down from heaven's glory to walk with you in your filth, to take it upon himself, all your iniquities and sins (like the book of Isaiah says) and nail it to the cross. The Bible says *"He who had no sin became sin"*. He takes our place and gives us life, hope, eternity; hope that when we die in a twinkle of an eye we will be with Him in eternity. He has taken everything that people have done or are ever going to do and nailed it to the cross; it all comes back to the cross. It is difficult as a human being to understand how hard it must have been when the Father turned His face from Jesus and Jesus said "it is finished". When all that stuff was going on, there was a separation of Father and Son on behalf of humanity so that we would have hope. The song 'In Christ Alone' conveys this message so well when it says "*Till on that cross as Jesus died, the wrath of God was satisfied*" (the wrath of God and the judgement of God never get spoken about).

The blood of Christ is so powerful that no matter what we may have done, where we have come from or whether we have been the biggest naughty rebellious one on planet earth, if we just say 'Jesus, I'm so sorry I have lived a life where I have been an abusive womaniser, a cultists, murder, a thief- forgive me for I have sinned', He would. This is why faith in prison is so powerful. These prisoners are not sitting in their comfortable homes and car, they have nowhere to go but to Jesus. It is a life-changing experience for them because they make a complete turnaround. It is a process for them because all of a sudden they get convicted of what they have done by the Holy Spirit nudging them in the chest. Before that, they were just happy in the murk but suddenly they have received the Messiah and their life changes. They see and feel things differently and this can sometimes be confusing. This is where the church needs to step in and help

13

these men who have received Christ and want to know about building the relationship with Him but don't know how or where to start. Many of them are carrying stuff that no one knows about, that they have not confessed publicly. They roll into the church expecting the church to welcome them and hear their stories but this is not often the case. The people they meet in the church look nothing like them, and sometimes people will try to relate with them using swear words but that is not what they want. They want to see a role model of Jesus not more of the same. And sometimes these men may not be just those coming from prisons, they could be men whose wives go to church and they stay at home because they 'can't get it'; there is nothing there (in church) for them. There is no attraction to church if Christ is not at the centre of it.

Any church that does not have the male camaraderie present will not work. Men like to stick together generally. Men need the camaraderie and sometimes women do not understand the need for this.

Pastors need to preach the truth

There is so much that needs to be preached, forgiveness, repentance, heaven is real, hell is real.

14

Pastors need to preach the truth. What the pandemic taught us is that 'Mickey Mouse' churches will not last. In Ezekiel 33: 6 it says "*But if the watchman sees the sword coming and does not blow the trumpet to warn the people and the sword comes and takes someone's life, that person's life will be taken because of their sin, but I will hold the watchman accountable for their blood.*' There is the urgency for preachers and evangelists, to challenge people to come to the cross because that is what the church should be about.

Simon recalls a time when he was speaking in a church at a men's breakfast and he asked the men if they could remember the date, time and place when they invited Jesus into their lives. His assumption was that since these were people who had been in church for a while this information would be etched on their hearts. Then one guy said he recalled a date in May 1980, which turned out to be the day when Ipswich beat Arsenal to win the FA Cup. He remembered that but not the date of his conversion. People need to know that coming to church for loads of years does not mean that you know Jesus. Going to Church is about the relationship with Jesus and surrendering everything to Him. Serving in the church for several years without accepting Jesus as Lord and saviour is all meaningless. The book of Isaiah 64:6 says our righteousness is like filthy rags *("But we are all as an unclean thing, and all our righteousness's are as filthy rags")* .Without a relationship with Jesus it is all pointless; get rid of all the stuff, all the nonsense and invite him into your life and submit and surrender to God.

Submission to God and bending the knee

Guys who are self-made men, who have their own business, find it hard to submit, because they are controllers and some have the nature within them to trample on others to get ahead. People are under the impression that when they bow their knees, they are surrendering. Men do not like it but surrendering to Christ brings freedom. There are different categories of men, blue-collar, men, in prisons and those who are comfortable at home. But men who are driven by constantly thinking about getting to the next stage and achieving more things, the ivory towers and building themselves a platform, have a syndrome called the 'greasy pole'. When they get to the top they don't know what to do because they feel empty. This happens a lot with men and then they start to look elsewhere for fulfilment and get involved in affairs, buying all sorts of things and doing things that no one knows about. They have access to what others do not have, they have a bit of a swagger and wonder why on earth they would need church. They are driven by their wants, the next new model TV or the next big car and that's how it keeps going and they get nowhere like a hamsters wheel. They spend years fighting their own selves and then decide to retire and feel it will be great. But many retired guys are lost, they have nothing going for them but what they have achieved, they have the motorbike, the place in the sun but they are still empty because all they have is external. The only thing that can fill that gap is Jesus but this means dying to self.

But dying to self does not mean you are weak or giving up, or can't have a few quid, you can but what is the purpose for your money, if you are striving to get the money and have no God purpose for it? It is pointless; striving for money is an endless journey that no one ever gets to the end of it. Some years ago on a chat show, Jonathan Ross and Will Smith were asked what their biggest fear was and they both said losing it all, losing the money. If that is driving you then you are in trouble. Having nothing but having Jesus, is everything, you don't need the riches of the world you need the richness of Christ, His presence and His Love, the love of Jesus.

17

However, even when people suddenly go through life realising that the body stops craving these things, they must remain mindful of the spiritual warfare that goes on in the mind so that they don't get caught back into that trap. This is why being grounded in the word is important, Galatians 2:20 is important it says, *"I have been crucified with Christ and I no longer live, but Christ lives in me. The life I now live in the body, I live by faith in the Son of God, who loved me and gave himself for me"*. Every morning we must put our flesh aside and not be weighed down by our emotions. The world feeds the flesh with 'gimme gimme gimme right now' messages but we are never going to beat the flesh.

We are in a world where it is all about 'me'

Motivational speakers tell you that you can do everything and even churches tell you that you can do all things through Christ. But people can do things with a verse taken out of context and sometime this verse is quoted out of context. **It is all about Jesus not about us**. So if we are using Jesus to write our story, then saying '**I**' can do all things is wrong. What we need to do is let Him write His story through us otherwise we are just using Jesus like a genie in a bottle

18

A lot of fine-sounding preachers are using scripture to build a business rather than focus on what their calling is. They feel that as pastors they can do everything but this is not the case. Dying to self becomes hard as they struggle with control. Many leaders focus on the individual but it is not about 'you' but about Jesus.

The prodigal son's story is so important

We often feel the grass is greener on the other side or that we can spend it, wine or dine it, but we can never be fulfilled, and may find ourselves eating with pigs. Sometimes the green grass is fake. But the Father's arms is always open; the love of a father is uncon-ditional.

We can say dad, 'I have been living a life that is so wrong' but He says "come son, come" – the wages of sin are death but the gift of God is eternal life. You can't ignore that. The world does not teach us to surrender. We are told that we can go out and do any-thing but when we come under Jesus we have to live by the word and it is not our will but His will. The world feels that it is free but it is bound up; true freedom is only in Christ. It is just like Thomas the Tank Engine who got off the rails (derailed) but kept

19

screaming I'm free. Don't get derailed, get back on the track, and stay with Jesus; that is freedom... that is the real freedom.

Men need to find their way back to Jesus, by walking with a real man, following Christ. Men need to walk with other men and talk with them. A real man will help them and lead them to the one who has the answers because we do not have the answers. It is about walking someone to Jesus and leaving them with Jesus and walking away.

We can all be an evangelist for Jesus, have a go for Jesus and find that one person that we can lead to Jesus.

Men in Church

I n this chapter we will be looking at men in general. In the book of, Jeremiah 51:30- it says *"Her mightiest warriors no longer fight. They stay in their barracks, their courage gone. They have become like women"* (NLT. He is talking about the Babylonian Army).

We will break this scripture into 4 parts

1. They Lost Their Fighting Spirit

The fighting spirit (not the spirit to go out and pick a fight but spiritual warfare), is not encouraged in men anymore.

Many men these days seem so lethargic in church and are doing nothing to the extent that the women are noticing. Simon recalls being asked by women to "come and fire up" their men. We are in a real situation when women begin to notice that men are battered. A talented young woman who played football for QPR and who also worked for the Billy

Graham association at the time, asked Simon to help her find a man. When he asked why, she commented that there were no 'real men' in her church. This is a sad indictment of where men are at the moment. Many men are looking good on the outside, driving the fancy cars but spiritually they are empty. It is the spiritual man that needs to rise in the UK. The reason we find ourselves in this situation is not because there is something wrong with the men but because the spiritual food has not been given out to them from the pulpit. The 'Las Vegas gospel' has been preached, the 'lights, glitz and glamour' message. But it is the gospel of Jesus that needs to be preached and the blood of Jesus. Unfortunately at the moment in the UK men feel like they have been beaten out of the church and are spiritually not alive.

Even though they are good men, because they do nothing, evil thrives. Whichever way we look at it the uncompromised gospel of Jesus Christ has to be preached. Because the gospel has not been preached to the church the men do not know how to be spiritual men. They have been taught a different gospel, such that we are looking at 'Gideon's' rather than 'David's' and encouragement does not come from the pulpit anymore. Rather, the Ted talkers are beating the drum, the motivational teachers are teaching a watered-down gospel, focusing on the feel-good factor – the adrenalin. This is why many men are hitting the gym trying to find this feel-good factor, trying to build themselves up externally. However, the main thing, which is building oneself spiritually, is neglected and the God-shaped hole is never filled. Men are trying to fill it with good stuff but if you are not fulfilled as a man you are always going to feel empty. Even though the outside looks good many men are broken on the inside and this becomes a distraction. The money, TV, and sports are distractions. Sports is a huge distraction because it is so easily accessible and can be watched 24/7 on different devices. With sports, you can sit and watch it all day and have a tee-shirt on with someone's name on your back living vicariously through that person. But if you do not play it, you can't get the fulfilment that comes from the sport.

Men need to start to fight back In Jesus name but they find it difficult. If men are not receiving the truth they will look in other areas and ultimately build on sand- **Don't build on sand build upon the Rock**. At this point in time, God is looking for a remnant of men who will stand up and say "I will have a go, I am not worried, I don't quite know where or what,

but I'll have a go".

It is a dangerous prayer to say when you say 'God use me', but it is exciting nonetheless. At first, it does not look like excitement because when you pray and ask God to use you, He will strip everything back so that the stuff that you have been looking at for spiritual fulfilment that does not give that fulfilment will start to be stripped away. We have to lay those things down, turn and go in a different direction. The world and society are all about self and motivational speakers prey on that and tell people 'you are great' their emphasis being on the 'You'. Even in the church people are told *'you can do all things through Christ who strengthens you, you are fearfully and wonderfully made'.* Although these scriptures are great, they are taken out of context, because we are **nothing** without Jesus and what He has done for us. But we are **everything** with Jesus and until we lay down 'self' every single day laying our flesh down to Jesus we will be unfulfilled. Unfortunately, the church has been infected by all the 'self, self' mantra. There does not seem to be a line in the sand between the world and church and it is all flowing in, the poison of the enemy is coming into the church.

The message here is not about bashing men, it is about encouraging them to be honest about how they feel and not to 'do it' alone. Instead, men should find a couple of like-minded men and do life with them, fellowship and discipleship. They are going through the same struggles. One thing that is common between men and which Simon has experienced several times is that at meetings when men gather you get many who say they never knew someone else was going through the same challenges as them. They also think the other fella has got it made because they focus on the outside impressions.

Men need to be encouraged to start the fight in Jesus name

2. *They Stayed in Their Stronghold*

Men today 'stay in' themselves focusing on their own selfish desires but it is time to step out in faith and be a Joshua and a Caleb. It's time to say 'with our God we are able'. It doesn't help that the present circumstances encourage people to stay indoors more and be locked down. The word lockdown is such a strong spiritual word that you can be locked in your building and also be locked down within yourself. And the more you are locked down the more anxious you become and depression and fear start to creep in.

You start to look at things and act differently. That stronghold is a strong spiritual one but if you know your Bible, your word, and you stand on it, you won't be frightened or fearful; you will go out. You will stand on your biblical values and will not compromise your faith. Men have to understand that they stand on the rock and build on Jesus and that as they build on Christ He is building them spiritually. As much as they build themselves physically, the Bible says in 1 Tim 4:8 *"For physical training is of some value, but godliness has value for all things, holding promise for both the present life and the life to come"*, so spiritual strength cuts across every area of life. Therefore, you can still enjoy the gym and all the other stuff but seeking first the kingdom of God and everything else will be added. When the spiritual man is built first everything else falls into place otherwise, if something else is more important than God then it is idolatry.

Unfortunately, men do not realise this is what is happening. They just see it as the culture and the way that they have been brought up, that you engage in the crowd and you bow. It is like worshipping Baal lifting up men and stuff over Christ. They don't realise that because it is a global phenomenon the devil uses it as a way to take men's eyes off Jesus. John Wimber the founder of the vineyard movement said: "show me where you put your energy, time and your money and I will show you what you worship". And in this day and age looking through someone's mobile phone and phone history will reveal what is number 1 in their life e.g. football, rugby, cars, even family. The priorities should be God, spouse, (if you are married), work, & ministry, that's it.

Many Christian men are distracted

There are so many Christian men whose lives are car crashes and when you ask what their priorities are and what time they are giving to the Lord, they say have not got time. Their priorities are all over the place, they have no time because they have to put Sky sports on and watch the big 'footy' on TV, or catch up on box sets etc. They are not willing to stay up to fast and pray but will stay up to watch a fight from Las Vegas. Many of them would probably go to church for a quick,' hello, how are you', 20 minutes worship and they run off to go home to watch sports or turn on the television. But there is an emptiness that runs along with that. The outside looks good but the inside is not. Priorities should be God, Spouse, Family, Work and Ministry. Sadly the suicide rate among men is high especially among men under 50. Recently a guy killed himself and the family knew nothing, they had no idea something was wrong. His outside looked good but his inside was broken. He could not share it because the culture of church and life does not let men share their feelings. It is all about 'bubbles and clouds and fluffy stuff'. Most men don't even know how to deal with their issues. Many times people are referred to counsellors but speaking with each other, knowing each other and having a conversation with each other can offer a release. Unfortunately, the enemy wants people to keep everything secret.

Men have lost the way of expressing themselves, like crying when they want to, they feel lost. Take the scenario of the corporate world, the men are so busy and have not time to attend their kids' events. Even though they want to attend the sports day, for example, the world of work does not allow it and they feel they have to stay 'thirsty' and bleed for the company but that is a lie. If that person left the next day, within 6 months he would be almost forgotten in the workplace and replaced. There are so many guys who get to work at 7am in the morning and do not leave until 7 pm and yet only get paid for a 8 hour job. They refuse to leave early because if they are seen to leave early they may appear weak or if they do not join in all the outings at work they may be seen as not sociable. But is amazing how Covid-19 has become a leveller and has made all those things to a degree seem meaningless. So these men have risen to the top of the corporate ladder and suddenly realise that they have missed out on other important stuff. These are good men who have just been misdirected.

So many Christian men who work in the city are also not able to express their faith, even though there are plenty of good churches that they could go to in the city. They have themselves tied to a big mortgage, their kids are in college, there is a massive financial commitment and they have become committed to a foreign god. They no longer find life exciting because of the daily grind and they can't even afford to die because of all the mortgages and re-mortgages etc. They are tied to all the trappings of the jobs e.g.

2 holidays a year etc. and suddenly they realise that they are not free but trapped. But he who the Son has set free is free indeed. It is great to have a good career and a good life but where is Christ in all of this? Sadly the teaching in the church does not emphasize Christ being the centre, so it is not the fault of these men but the teaching.

There are a lot of women in the church whose husbands do not come to church because there is no excitement for them there -nothing for the men. Simon used to run a local gym for adults and there were a lot of men who would come into the gym on their way from work. One of them was made redundant and he was panicking about it but he started to do some gardening and got some clientele. Even though he did not have as much money as he used to, he looked 10 years younger because he was no longer under the stress of life- the 'hamster wheel' of life. He was able to put more time into his faith and was blossoming. When asked if he would ever go back, he said no.

Where one works is also important. If one is locked down in a building all day it is not good for the soul. The guy who became a gardener was working outdoors and had creation all around him and it changed his thoughts; there is something to be said for that. If you are looking down the lens of a screen all day in a box, it is not good.

The enemy ties self-worth to cars, jobs, houses etc. and if you buy into that stuff you lose your identity completely, it is like putting a massive chain around yourself. Identity is lost because it is in those things and outside of Christ. People are identified by what they earn, you hear all the time "how much do earn" etc. and when you look at these things it is meaningless 'moth and rot'. As it says in Ecclesiastics it is meaning-less.

3. Their Courage had Gone

We are living in very powerful biblical times and God is speaking to men and they are finding it foreign. But the thing is, how does one hear God's voice? , if you are not in your word, studying and meditating on the word of God you cannot hear His voice. God is saying "I am talking to you but you cannot hear me because you are full of all this other stuff, you are not in my word and not recognising what I am saying" It says in the Bible my sheep will know my voice, so, if you are in the Bible and fellowshipping the right way, and you are getting into the spirit of the word you will hear God. If you let the noise of the world get to you, it will affect you. This is why every man needs to be careful of outside voices.

If you spend time unplugged from the phone and all the gadgets, speaking to God, that quiet time with God will be absolutely precious and a life changer. Even in Ministry as Pastor Ben notes, it can be overbearing and it can lead you down the wrong rabbit hole. What men should do is what Pastor David Wilkerson of Cross and Switchblade fame says- everyone should find time for a private closet, find a time when there is no distraction and just get on one's knees before the Lord, praising and worshipping. If you do that you will hear from the Lord. Being spiritually still in addition to the physical stillness will help you connect with God *"Be still and know that I am God"*.

We are in a society that wants everything now, the 'Blink' society but Isaiah 40 :31 says *"But they that wait upon the LORD shall renew their strength"*; that means time, waiting takes time. Unfortunately, people want to go to a church where they will be zapped by the Spirit, they don't want to take the time to read the Bible; they want the instant results now. But there is no shortcut to reading the Bible. When you follow Jesus it will be hard, because it is like swimming upstream. But Isaiah in the same scripture talks about lost courage being restored. If you have lost your courage you will not step out, you will be comfortable and because society has got you caught in a crowd, you can't afford to step out and you end up being a robot; a nice comfortable man. However, there is more to get from the Christian faith. It is easy to praise the Lord when everything is going great but praising when everything has gone wrong, when there is no money or the relationship has broken down, is hard. It is difficult to find the position of praise when your courage is lost unless you know God.

32

MEN IN CHURCH

Many men are afraid of how they are perceived when they say that they are following Jesus, many of them say that they don't let people at work know they are Christians, they prefer to be closet Christians and have allowed the enemy to isolate them. They are too afraid to come out and be seen. Simon encourages men to have a go for Jesus, this means saying at work, 'I go to church, I was in church on Sunday', instead of skirting around the issue of church and letting people know where they stand. Men should raise their flag for Jesus and tell people about Him whenever they can. Men could start conversations when asked what they do by saying "I worship Jesus". The enemy has done a great job of presenting Jesus as a weak character but men have to start smashing that image and telling people that Jesus is the King of glory, the lion of Judah, the strongest man that ever lived. They must tell people that they are Jesus followers. When people know how powerful Christ is, they can do all things. That is what the scripture "I can do all things through Christ means", the scripture is about getting behind Jesus and going through the door as He opens it. It is not about you but Christ's ability to strengthen you. It is about Jesus, so keep your eyes fixed on Him, scripture says to keep your eyes fixed on the author and finisher of our faith- Jesus.

33

In a church in the area where Simon lives, men are challenged to go out and have a go for Jesus. It was slow at first but slowly people began to tell their colleagues at work that they went to church and some were even saying 'God bless you' to the 'lady at Costa'... having a go for Jesus. They were no longer ashamed to admit that they spent Sunday in church. People started to get excited about introducing Jesus in their conversations. It was no longer about going to church on Sunday but living out for Jesus daily, living for Christ 24/7. Real men are being encouraged to live for Christ 24/7. Men must not be afraid to tell people about Jesus because there is power in that name. When you start to speak the name of Jesus, the body loses all fear, the mind disappears and the greatness of God starts to rise within you because it is supernatural. The Bible encourages us not to be ashamed because it says if we are ashamed of Jesus, He will be ashamed of us; that is a scary thought.

Having a go for Jesus is not about being a freaky Christian but being sensible with discernment. Just live for Jesus, not the church, the institution or the work, just for Jesus and your life will be transformed. Your life will be exciting because you will wake up anticipating who God will bring across your path so that you can talk to them about Jesus. You will still get on with your daily life, but with Jesus at the centre. And your colleagues at work who may have been ridiculing you will come to you first when they have a problem because you are living for Jesus.

The important thing to think about is mortality. When you die where are you going? Unfortunately, people focus on the adrenalin rush of things around them but you can have an adrenaline rush, living for Jesus, interrupting your day just to live for Him, sowing the seed about Jesus.

4. They had become like Women

This does not mean that women are weak. The Bible says the man is the head of the household, the spiritual head. However, men have abdicated their role and have allowed women to take the lead. Men have not fulfilled their biblical responsibilities as men. The men as the head of the family should be standing in the gap for their families but they are not doing what they should and the women have had to take charge because most men are sitting on their backsides too consumed with their busy lives and busy jobs, watching sports. The men of today are not necessarily weak but what is critical is the message they receive from the altar. The men on the inside of them need to be strengthened. Men are not present in the situation so the wives or women do everything and the men do not take their place. It is okay for the women to be amazing prayer warriors but the man has to be the shield of protection for his family that they can stand behind. The man is the one who should be fixing stuff for the family. **The 3 most important words women want to hear is not 'I love you', but 'I'll do that'.** Unfortunately, men are such procrastinators, they are great at saying 'leave it I'll do it' and 3 months later it is still not done that the women often get frustrated by it all. The men seem too busy all the time and sometimes get consumed socialising too much that they forget the important things. The enemy uses the world of sports, the pub etc. to keep men from doing what they should be doing.

The only way a man can get himself right is with Jesus being the centre. When building up a family the most important things are not the IPads and gadgets but example, example, example. Children copy what they see, so they mirror what is in front of them. Although men do not have many role models, the ultimate role model to follow is Jesus. Who we follow is important. The world tries to encourage us to follow a man, but no man is greater than the other. Even in the world of the church, you get people asking what this pastor or this leader, thinks about stuff, but it is not about them because if you watch a man and follow him very closely you will be disappointed. All a man can do for you is to guide you to Jesus. According to Pastor Ben, he often tells people not to come to church to see him but Jesus. The church which he oversees is not about him but Jesus, the Messiah. But what we see is a culture that lifts men. Although it is good to encourage people and support one another, no man must be put in the place of a god. For instance, when people recommend one book or the other to you, it is better to read the Bible for yourself because you can get all of it in the Bible. Many ministries try to produce literature that is greater than Matthew, Mark, Luke and John, or Genesis to Revelation and focus on a 'vision' and all this amounts to is someone's interpretation of the Bible. But just sharing the word and giving out the Bible is very powerful. There have been doctors and nurses who have been given Bibles and have later come back to ask more questions about Jesus. Ministries do not need to produce a pack of some grand style literature when they can just give the Bible. All this literature has a shelf life but the Bible has survived from generation to generation. The word remains the same ... *"in the beginning was the Word and the Word was God"*. The word has to be at the beginning of everything. So whilst giving of literature is often about 'bigging the author up', giving out the word, the Bible, is all about Jesus. There are indeed anointed men and women who have the gift to write Christian literature but these must not be taken over the word of God because nothing can take that place. The word has got to be at the centre, if not you are on the wrong path. The Bible says *seek ye first the kingdom of God*, if you do not know the scriptures how can you make sense of it all? The Bible says "*my people perish for lack of knowledge*". The knowledge referred to here is not just educational knowledge but educational acknowledgement through the word of God.

The Bible has everything in it that a man needs for marriage, finances, life, business, culture correction, rebuke, everything, it is almost like a no brainer. In 2nd Tim 3:16-17 it says, "*All Scripture is God-breathed and is useful for teaching, rebuking, correcting and training in righteousness, so that the servant of God may be thoroughly equipped for every good work*" (NIV). Equipped for every good work, being equipped is the keyword because although the literature may sound good it does not fill one up as the scripture does.

Accepting Jesus as Lord and saviour is the first step but we must follow Jesus back to the father. Not knowing his biological father Simon felt that he needed a spiritual father. So he would look for guys or pastors who would be a 'spiritual director' for him. But his wife would always question the need for this spiritual father. As far as she was concerned he did not need a spiritual father when he already has the Father.

Over the years there has been a drive for accountability and hence the issue of a spiritual father. Although accountability is necessary, when you call someone your spiritual father you are driving someone's ego and putting enormous pressure on them. The only person to have as a spiritual father is God; man is man. You can go to any man and he will listen to you but there is a limit to what they can do for you. The structure of pastors and leadership is good but these men/women must lead you to the Father through Jesus. It is important to understand that we are accountable to Christ, the King of Kings and Lord of Lords. And although there are layers to the church structure above everything else we are accountable to Christ. Being accountable to each other is important James 5:16 says to confess to one another *("Therefore confess your sins to each other and pray for each other so that you may be healed")*. But this does not replace following Jesus

Since the Garden of Eden, God has been waiting for men to come back to Him. He sent prophets and Jesus to lead people back to the Father. Repentance and acceptance of Jesus alone is not enough, it must lead you back to the Father without question. That is the only way. Jesus said "*I am the way* and *the truth and the life*. No one comes to the Father except through me" (John 14:6); He did not need a spiritual director. There comes a time in life when you have to journey alone with Christ. Your pastor can only go so far with you, your bishop can get you to another level but there comes a point that you have to walk only with Jesus. All the gifted men and women in the spirit are only gifted because God has gifted them but they can only feed your flesh and the Father hates self. We are here to do the Father's will and that is why following Jesus and not just walking with Him is so important.

Sadly, we live in a time where not only is there a virus pandemic and a spiritual one, there is also a pandemic of fatherless children within our society. We need a spiritual father and desperately need the guidance of our King of glory. Above Covid-19, the world is looking for a father, there are children out there without fathers and women have had to take the lead. We live in a time where men are going around creating babies with several 'baby mamas'. Thank

God for the earthly fathers, pastors and ministers but there is a limit to how one can grow just with these leaders. There is a scripture in the book of Corinthians which says *"For even if you had ten thousand others to teach you about Christ, you have only one spiritual father. For I became your father in Christ Jesus when I preached the Good News to you."*.

Louis Theroux had 5 or 6 black guys with him who had all been in trouble with the police, when he asked for their father they laughed and said their mum was their father. Also somewhere in Africa, there was a herd of elephants that had gone wild, when they studied why, it was discovered that all the big male elephants had been killed off so there was no structure. This is what is happening in society today. Men have abdicated their positions to the women and are sitting back. The enemy uses that very cleverly to degrade all humanity, using men against women. The Father's plan was a family, man, woman and children, Adam and Eve not Adam and Steve but the enemy has smashed that plan in so many ways. So the spiritual father can only be Jesus. When we put our trust in a person, no matter how godly, they are limited still. But Jesus is not limited, He endless.

There is a story that dates back to President Lincoln in the American Civil War. A soldier was waiting to

41

see President Lincoln because he wanted to leave the army and he waited for days and Abraham Lincoln did not have time to see him. Then a little boy showed up and asked him what he was doing and he told him that he was waiting for Lincoln, and the little boy said, 'follow me'. He took him through all the other soldiers and straight to the president. And the president asked what he wanted and the little boy told him the man wanted to see him. The little boy was the President's Son. This is the same with Jesus, we can follow Him and He will take us straight to the throne room of the Father. When you know the love of the Father you do not want anything else. You never want to go away from His love or feel abandoned by God. When you feel that, you know exactly what God felt when He saw his Son on the cross. It is difficult to understand that.

It is necessary to appreciate and respect our earthly fathers and the church fathers but they are limited as to what they can teach. We can get direction from all these people but knowing the truth is what sets one free. If we look at the prodigal son, the father was waiting for his son to come back despite everything. He did not question, where he'd been, who he had been sleeping with or where the money had gone, he just said 'my son is home'. That's all that matters to the father. The Love of Jesus is amazing but the love of the Father is different. Most men relate their relationship to the Father with their experience with their earthly father's and if that relationship has been fragmented, it is difficult to understand this Father God who loves them. We point these men to Jesus and Jesus leads them to the Father. Jesus says He is the way the truth and the life, no one comes to the Father except through Him. Jesus seeks to do the will of the Father. It is all through Jesus. Those men finding it hard to understand the heavenly Father can follow Jesus, by reading the Bible and Jesus will lead them to the Father.

The biggest challenge the church leaders could ever have is getting rid of all literature and just having Bibles because the Bible is all we need. Literature, your pastor and your earthly father will get you so far but no one can get you into heaven except Jesus. So why waste time reading literature that man has written over the greatest book in the world? The disciples did not worry about this book or that book or some podcast or the other they were mainly interested in the words of Jesus. There are massive bestsellers across the world that is simply a regurgitation of the Bible from some-one's perspective. It is much better to get a Bible and a good concordance and dig in yourself. It would be interesting to go home and for a whole year, close down every piece of literature and just stay in the word for 12 months being guided by the Holy Spirit. With the help of the Holy Spirit, it becomes revelation and just jumps out at you. *"All Scripture is given by inspiration of God, and is profitable for doctrine, for reproof, for correction, for instruction in righteousness, that the man of God may be complete, thoroughly equipped for every good work".* 2Tim 3:16-17 (NKJV). If you spend a whole year in the word you will be fully equipped.

It is necessary to evaluate how much time we spend in the word and how much time we spend on TV, or other pursuits, social media etc. It will give perspective on how much time you spend to feed your spirit. There is a story of a man that dreamed of the evil dog and the good dog always fighting but he never got to the end of the story. He asked a wise man who he thought would win and the man said 'it is the one you feed the most that wins'. What are you feeding your spirit with? what is on TV can darken your spirit. A lot of it is satanic and occultism. Watch what your children are watching, be very careful what you allow to go into you. The Bible *says "out of your belly shall flow rivers of living water"* (John 7:38) but it is what you feed yourself that you will become.

So just read the word, men read the word, lay all the literature aside, stop chasing after this ministry or that ministry and just follow the greatest leader of all Jesus. It is all about Jesus.

The Perception of Jesus

The world has a certain perception of Jesus; we cannot switch on the TV without hearing the name of Jesus used as a swear word, an exclamation and a curse word etc. It is really interesting to see how the name of Jesus is sometimes used as a curse word globally. If someone caught their hand in the door you won't hear them say 'oh Mohammed or oh Buddha', it is always Jesus. The enemy knows that it is the most powerful full name because at the name of Jesus every knee bows. Whatever culture you are from, wherever you are and you hurt yourself or there is a problem or you are cursing, it is always the name of Jesus. It is so popular now that you only need to switch on the television. It is used so fluidly just as a causal word and people interject a swear word with the name of Jesus. This is a sign of the times that we live in today. If you are a Christian man and that does not hurt you then there is a problem.

So how do we see Jesus? From Ben's perspective, Jesus can be seen the way He is portrayed on the cross in films etc. but it is more than that. He says "I see Him carry my pain my anger, my frustration worries and doubts. I see Him as a risen saviour as well. I see Him resurrected as the king of glory".

The strongest Man that ever lived

Sadly, we have an enemy who is a liar and an imitator and he has done a great job of taking the image of Jesus and turning it into a Ned Flanders type of character, a weak character that is frail. And schools are not teaching about Jesus anymore so people are growing up just knowing Jesus as a swear word. We have to address that and do so now, so that we can show people that Jesus was the strongest man that ever lived and the only perfect man in every area of His life. In everywhere that He walked and in everything that He did, he was strong, confrontational and did not shy away from any stuff - He engaged it.

Some churches and ministries ride on the back of social justice, feeding the homeless and sheltering people and cling to the feeble image of Jesus and will champion that. But Jesus never came to change that, He never came to stop slavery, cure poverty, social or racial injustice but what He did do was to change the hearts of people setting captives free. Once you change the heart of someone then everything else will follow. It is amazing to feed the needy and look out for people but all of these things have to be done in the name of Jesus. Not in the name of religion or social justice but in a biblical way and in the way Christ would want us to. So being a man for Christ, as we look at His humanity, we see that He is not frail, He had strength. These days when people talk about strength they refer to the physical body as a perfect body, looking like Popeye, popping out everywhere, chest pumped out all that sort of stuff but Christ was strong in a different way. There is a difference between Spiritual strength and physical strength. 2nd Tim says *"physical exercise is good for a little bit spiritual strength is good for everything"*.

William Booth founder of the Salvation Army said you can take a man out of the gutter, you can feed and clothe him and then send him to hell because you do not tell him the truth about the gospel of Jesus Christ. It has to be Jesus first, the greatest words that can be shared with humanity is that Jesus loves them. He died on the cross for you, he set you free and has given you a hope and a future and everything else will follow that pathway. Once you turn that heart around everything else will change because it is a heart thing.

THE PERCEPTION OF JESUS

As we know, *"the heart is deceitful above all things, and desperately wicked: who can know it?"*(Jeremiah 17: 9) and the book of Mathew tells of 13 things that come out of the heart all negative things. If you try and deal with this stuff on your own you will never win. You will keep going around in circles feeding the flesh. The flesh is full of lust and anger etc. and it has to be made clear that even when you start following Christ all of you doesn't just automatically get all this stuff. You don't immediately become some sort of 'holy Joe' floating on a cloud to the office. When you become a disciple of Jesus, what you begin to notice is a conviction of the Holy Spirit, but you will have the natural knack from of the body and the lust of the flesh. The Bible makes it very clear it says *"the spirit is willing but the flesh is weak"*. So suddenly where you did not have any moral understanding of what was right and wrong to a certain degree, as soon as you become a born again believer in Christ, you get the power of God that brings you under conviction and then you have a bigger challenge than you will ever face because you are battling yourself, and the reason for this battle is because you now have Christ in you. Paul in one of his many letters said "it's Christ in me" Galatians 2:20, *(" I have been crucified with Christ and I no longer live, but Christ lives in me. The life I now live in the body, I live by faith in the Son of God, who loved me and gave himself for me"*). You are convicted all the time. If anyone says that they do not have any struggles they are lying, that cannot be true. When you give yourself to Christ your spiritual eyes are open and you start to think 'oh my God, I was feeding the flesh and living on adrenalin. I was living in fear and for addictions and it has become my natural way of life and I was trying to feed the beast- the flesh'. Feeding the flesh is our biggest enemy because we are fighting ourselves. We wake up with bruises because we have been fighting ourselves and are our own biggest enemies. We think we can sort these things out ourselves so we give in to them and think it is freedom. We think we are free to do this and that but all the time that is a lie of the enemy because he is keeping us in bondage to that stuff.

The door has been open to men at a very young age to pornography. Everything has been sexualised and you only have to listen to, or watch the TV, or even look at posters. Everything has a sexual connotation and men and women on social networks all have to have the perfect body. It is the lust of the flesh, the Jezebel spirit. Ahab should never have married Jezebel. He was serving the God of Israel and she was serving Baal. When you look at that marriage, you find that Jezebel had a more strong influence over Ahab because it was all lust. They got involved in all kinds of perversion imaginable but now all these things have become part of everyday life. The media and the internet promote it so much.

While ministering at a church a sometime ago a guy approached Simon and thanked him for the message saying that he needed to hear it. He said that he and his wife watched Love Island all the time. This was a Christian man watching that stuff. Unfortunately, because the message of the gospel of Jesus has not come over the pulpit about the blood and condemnation and repentance, people feel comfortable doing anything. The church has watered the message down saying that grace covers it all so you can watch what you like and there is no correction anymore. So with love island etc., it has become normal, and people sit and watch all sorts of stuff on TV. But it is nothing new and comes out of Baal worship and worship of the fertility gods from the Old Testament. It drove the Israelites wild.

When Moses was up on the mountain speaking to God, the Israelites could not wait. They started to have orgies and do all manner of things, seeking foreign gods and idolatrous worship. Because the flesh is powerful, they were getting drunk; this is nothing new. Pornography is not hidden anymore it is on the posters and kids TV. The thing is the world is getting more and more of it so the moral bar is being lowered even more. It is like the story of the frog in water, if you put a frog in hot water it will jump straight out but if you put it in cold water and slowly heat it, it will stay there. So these evil things have become normalised, whereas few years ago you would not have heard the name of Jesus being used as a blasphemous word, and you would not get 2 men or 2 women kissing on television, now it is the norm, and if it is not included in the program, then it is regarded as a bigoted program. One cannot watch anything on TV without seeing all of this stuff and they keep pushing it more and more each day. On the other hand, it is becoming hard to see families consisting of mum, dad and kids on TV (which is God's plan). The family has been or is being pushed out because it is biblical and the enemy wants to kill, steal and destroy that. He has destroyed the image of Jesus, but if we look at what Jesus said and how he went about His life we will find that Jesus was confronting all leaders and systems of the time. In Matt23:1-39 Jesus said that they occupied all the best seats of the temple, they had everything but tied cumbersome loads on others but they were not willing to lift a finger themselves.

They tried to catch Him out several times, once when they brought an adulterous woman before Him He did not even look at them but said something quite amazing. Thus, the guy who is perceived to be a weak person said: *"He who is without sin, let Him cast the first stone"* and one by one they walked away. He confronted these leaders without any anger or drama. Then he said to the woman, your sins have been forgiven, go away and sin no more. The Bible tells us that all have sinned and come short of the glory of God but beyond that is the power of forgiveness that Jesus expressed here.

Jesus is our God and king but the church dresses Him up in a manger and tosses Him out at Christmas and it does not help. We must be standing up and declaring that Jesus was the strongest man who died on the cross.

When the religious leaders kept trying to test Him, He said to them *"who the Son sets free is free indeed"* and then he went on to accuse them that their father is the devil, the father of lies. So Jesus was literally across the table from these guys and accusing them.

So here we have this Christ figure, no gym involved, no steroids involved, no influence of any physical impression of some pumped up guy and we see Christ using the power of speech, the word of God and scripture, just speaking without getting angry. And although we have an example in the Bible where we see Jesus overturning the tables of the money changers and getting a whip, in this instance, He displays the strength and the power that He had to just speak. This is the Son of God in the flesh living as a human being. He has come down from heaven and humbled himself. He stooped down and became a servant and because of that the Father exalted Him and it says in 2 Philippians, *Jesus is the most powerful name in the whole of the universe, in the history, and at the name of Jesus* every *knee will bow*- there is power in the name of Jesus and yet this name is being used and abused all over society.

In the story of Shadrach, Meshach and Abednego, we are told they refused to bow their knee to the king; they stood for what they believed in. They said "whether we live or die we will not bow our knees". (But culture is trying to get us to bow our knees to so many things). The enemy has paralysed Christian men and they are stuck to their seats and don't realise they have the most powerful name, the greatest name in heaven and on earth. God gave Him a name above every other that at the name of Jesus every knee would bow, on earth, under the earth and every tongue shall confess Jesus Christ is Lord.

Yet these guys in the church are blinded and must have muffles over their ears; their hearts are hardened and seared, they are so paralysed and just sitting there. Before the pandemic, the church was just a Sunday morning club that they went to. They did not realise that by accepting Jesus Christ as Lord and Saviour that they have now got the power of Christ living in them. (They did not realise that they are powerful men). It has nothing to do with physical stature or the number of times spent in the gym, because *"greater is He that is in me than he that is in the world"* (1 John 4:4)

It is not the fault of the men but that of the church.

The church has not preached Matthew, Mark, Luke and John, it has not preached creation, eschatology, the rapture of the church and it has flapped around the skirt of satan; it has not pressed the gospel. If the gospel and the blood of Christ had been spoken about e.g. repentance, sin, hell's hot, heaven's real, if they preach the real gospel of Jesus it will open up the spiritual eyes of people. However, if you have a motivational word coming out, it will get your feathers fluffed a little bit and make you feel good, and that is simply adrenalin and not the Spirit of God.

This is not a popular message; telling people that if they do not repent that they are going to hell is not preached. But a watered-down gospel is preached and the prosperity gospel has been cleverly preached. Many motivational speakers manipulate people and talk about money and emphasise that people should give a tithe, a wave offering, a blow offering or a stand on your hand offering, all manner of offerings etc. and all of these just feed the flesh because money is attractive. But Jesus said to the disciples, drop your nets and follow me, bring nothing with you, follow me and I shall supply.

Beware of false doctrines

There was a guy in a church who had been divorced and remarried, and his church used him to speak from time to time. He said that he had a 1 bedroom flat somewhere in case he was tempted to flirt again. But he said it was okay to do so and he was saying he knew he could be forgiven because everything has been covered by grace. But you cannot be 80% faithful to your wife it is all or nothing. This is an example of the watered-down 'grace covers all' gospel. Because that is telling you that you can do what you like, and this comes off the back of the scripture that asks how many times can one be forgiven, 70x 7 times? and they talk about the prodigal son, so it is almost giving humanity the license to go out and live the dream, cross genders, come back, jump in bed with him or her, wake up the dog and the cat do whatever you want.

Although forgiveness is powerful, this false doctrine gives the impression that people can do whatever they like without any consequences of sin. But God does not wink at sin. You cannot come in and go out of the church and continue living the same way. Forgiveness only comes with repentance which is a turning away.

Sin is a turning away from God's will for you. There are very few sermons these days that make people stop and think about how they live their lives. Many people barely even remember the sermon, those who might remember might do so till about Tuesday of that week and then it is gone.

There is power in the name of Jesus

There was a guy who had accepted Jesus into his life. On the night he had accepted Jesus into his life he had already made a note in his diary to kill himself that day, what a turnaround that was- what an amazing story. This guy was an ex-boxer, plumber. He was struggling with the ex-husband of his wife and he had every intention to harm that ex-husband the next time he came round to cause trouble. But when the ex-husband came round, shouting and swearing, he just asked the guy if he wanted to meet Jesus and go to church with him. The ex-husband was stopped in his tracks and immediately fell into the arms of this guy and started crying. He said "mate, I just need something, I am so angry".

The power in the name of Jesus hit him at the right time, the most vulnerable time, when anger, guilt, frustration and the flesh was driving. The battle belongs to the Lord. There is so much power in the name.

The world is angry, fearful, lost, and needs a saviour.

The men in the church are lost because the leaders have not driven the word. And where the church is focused on outreach to the secular world, it feels like the church has to become the world to win the world. That is the norm now such that the church adopts the pattern and business models of the world with the pie charts, bar charts etc. and everything is measured. This is more popular because many churches are expanding daily in big numbers, because they are following a business model/ some formula and the driving factor is money because money opens doors. According to Pastor Ben, the first time he meets someone from another church the first question they ask is "how many people are in your Church" and that is usually the focus of many people. He simply answers "four of us, Father, Son, Holy Ghost and I, if any human being rolls in today that's fine".

It is about number crunching; it is almost like the higher the number, the greater the church leader is. That is what a lot of church leaders are doing. They are taking the system of 'I am great', 'I am', and everything points to the pulpit and the guy at the front of the church. So who is at the top of the tree? it is certainly not Jesus, but the man with the white teeth and leather jacket, driving the fast motorbike and all the cars etc. and he is on YouTube every week preaching. But what is the preaching about? It's about 'self', it's all about what you can be. Most of these motivational speakers or preachers, life-coaches and spiritual directors adopt a Ted talk approach and quote scripture out of context 'my God shall supply all my houses and Mercedes in Jesus name' they quote scripture like *"cast your bread upon many waters and it will return", "the battle belongs to the Lord"* etc. and manipulate it and the human ears love it. One can take the context of scripture and manipulate it and then the gospel becomes watered down. Before Covid-19, faith healers were all over the place saying God's healed you of cancer, your leg has grown, throw your wheelchair away but the moment the pandemic hit, these faith healers went into hiding. If God is healing them why are they running from Covid?.

The Bible in 1st John 2:16 talks about the lust of the eyes, the lust of the flesh and the pride of life. The pride of life is what we are dealing with here and the pride of life in this context is the word of faith that centres on 'you'. The word that says 'don't give up, you're the best, you're the centre and you are in every place in the Bible, you're David'... but you are not. Because the Father has got one plan that has not changed in two thousand years and that is salvation through Jesus. We are nothing without Jesus and even Jesus said I can do nothing without the father.

The word became flesh and made His dwelling among us. We have the God of Israel come to the world and He chose the dressing room of Mary's womb to pop out into this world. *"In the beginning was the Word, and the Word was with God, and the Word was God,"* but suddenly Christ says I can do nothing without Him, but He (Christ) is the word. This is mind-blowing when you think about it.

We can do nothing without Jesus

Men have to get a grip on this fact that Jesus said He is the vine; they are grafted into the vine and can do nothing apart from Him. So without Christ, they can only go so far because although we can build certain things, our life is like a Lego block. As we build we are building structure but the structure has its place. We can build structure in the form of business, culture and life but without the breath of God and the spirit of God, it is nothing. It won't and can't get anyone into heaven. We might get a pat on the back from other guys but that is it. The world has adopted culture from Darwin, which encourages people to trample on anyone and crush anyone they need to just to get to the top, 'survival of the fittest'. It has become so bad now that if people have diverging views from that of the world they are thrown out of the window. If you disagree with all the different transgender stuff for example you are regarded as bigoted, and the world says you hate those people. If you don't bend the knee to this, or that, you are against popular opinion and your opinion does not matter.

This is why men in Christ have to stand up, because of the persecution. There is serious oppression on them by the world. There may be some men who don't care and are content sitting on their sofa doing nothing and that's okay. But for those men and women who want to do more and stand out for Christ, those who are hungry for Christ, they should know that God will use them wherever they are. He wants the name of Jesus to be glorified, worshipped and to be out there. God wants strong Christian men, the remnant, to work together, disciple each other and stand up for Him. He has had enough of the paralysed, lukewarm men. He wants men that will be on fire for him men who want to walk with Jesus. Following Jesus is a great thing to do, you don't need money, you don't need to be an educator, and you don't need anything. He just wants your heart. He died for you.

John Piper gave a sermon and talked about a Christian couple who after retirement went around collecting shells. When they died God asked them what they had been doing and they said collecting shells and God responded, I have enough shells, what I want are souls and not shells.

Pornography

The topic of pornography is not preached in church and yet it is a massive struggle for guys in the church. It causes, depression, breaks up marriages, ruins relationships, takes men out and causes untold pain and some even commit suicide because of it. There is a myth that pornography does not exist in the church and that everyone in the church is holy "and we can't talk about that". But we have a generation of men who have been looking at this stuff since they were teens especially because of the easy access to it.

It is not new

Pornography is not new, if you go back into the Old Testament it was as real as it is today and it was everywhere. You will find that there were orgies and all manner of absurdities. There is nothing new under the sun, all the pornography, the lust of the flesh, is not new but what has happened is that it is more available to the eyes today. We look at the life of Lot who was attracted by Sodom and Gomorrah and all the wealth that he could get, and there was also sexual perversion going on there too. Man has gone all the way in this and it is something that the enemy uses in secret. It isolates men and makes them feel bad, dirty and guilty.

Access via the internet makes it easier for people to obtain it. Years ago, it was 'top shelf stuff' not easily accessible. Men used to exchange magazines as young men but the sexual perversion has gone to another level these days. The sexual perversion of the Canaanites, serving of fertility gods and all the orgies that can be found in the Bible was a common way of life then. Today, culture, TV, advertisements, have made it almost a normal way of life. There are so many platforms through which young kids and everyone can access pornography. This is not mainly a male issue because even women have issues with pornography too. There are all sorts of programs like Love Island etc. that can be classified as soft porn. Almost daily, it is in your face even in the 'normal' programs you watch; billboards carry adverts that promote pornography. The human eyes cannot seem to get away from it whether you are a man or a woman. And for those who take a step further and click on pornographic stuff, it becomes addictive.

God's design for mankind is for a man to be attracted to a woman, engage with her and form a family, but the enemy is destroying that. Any man or woman out there who has children, ask yourself, were your children conceived in lust or love?, because lust takes and love gives. Unfortunately, we have a society where many children were conceived in lust. The Bible makes it clear that all have sinned and fallen short of God's glory. Each man is drawn away by his lust for the flesh; there is a pull in everyone towards something that attracts towards what feeds the flesh. When we talk about children born in love or lust, it is because the world has pushed lust. The world promotes lust and not love; it is a 'taking world'. It is about a quick, rumble in the jungle, a quick, 'crash bang wallop man', everything is quick just feeding the flesh. Everything the world pushes is adrenalin rushing, lust, the quick fired stuff; the world is living for instant gratification and worldly pleasure; that was also evident in the Old Testament. Moses had gone up to the mountain to be with God, where he had his countenance change etc. and when he came back down full of the glory of God, his people were at it like rabbits at the bottom of the mountain, having orgies and drunk. It is nothing new, but with time it has become more acceptable and is in plain sight. The filth that comes out of Hollywood is unbelievable. Simon watched The Designated Survivor on Netflix, the first 2 series were okay, no swearing, no sex, but by the 3rd series it had all changed. Netflix also promoted a film called Cuties about young children for which there has been an outcry. Although this is unbelievable, it happened in the past too. In the Old Testament, people were selling their children for prostitution, but now we have it dressed up.

There is a root to everything, a root of anger and one of pornography too.

The root of pornography is intimacy, the lack of intimacy. The intimacy God wants is that between a man and a woman (which is beautiful), but the enemy who is an imitator is promoting the lust of the eyes making people look at stuff. You have a young man who starts looking at this stuff slowly and then this opens a door and he becomes hooked. What happens is that it distorts completely how the relationship with a female should be. All of a sudden you can't have sex normally because you're driven and your motivation and libido is driven by what you see. You feel she has to be like this and look like that and be doing this or that. A normal relationship is out of the window, and all of a sudden you can't perform in a normal relationship and you become depressed and miserable. Some get so bound up by all of this, they take Viagra, are on anti-depressants and some even commit suicide because they can't figure a way out. Suicide is the biggest killer of men under 50 in the UK. This is a subject that the church disregards and does not talk about. It is easy to get into but very difficult to get out of because it is driven by a dark side to it.

So you have the battle of the flesh because it feeds the eyes and the mind and the natural perception. By the time you leave the church and are minding your business driving home, the way people dress and the advertisements, all bring it in your face. If you are breathing on earth you cannot escape the way the enemy uses the media to promote sex. Over the years there has been a 'softly, softly' approach such that now it has become the norm. Even with social media, the more filthy, or degrading you are with your posts the more you seem to be accepted; it is almost like a competition.

A few years ago Simon's son had gone out with a girl on 3 occasions and had not had sex with her. His friends called him gay because of that. The thing is, God is not surprised at people having sex…He invented sex. Sex in the right context of marriage is a beautiful thing, an amazing thing, where couples give love to each other. But the enemy has changed that.

Pornography exists in the church!!

The issue with pornography is rife in churches. In one of the men's meetings where Simon was ministering a while back, a well-dressed man, who was part of the ministering team approached him and asked for prayer because according to him, he looked at pornography once every 2 weeks. At a different conference, during the coffee break, the guy on the sound deck came forward to ask for prayers because he had been looking at pornography the night before. He knew he was coming to a Christian conference the next day but he just could not stop himself from watching pornography. It has been programmed in the minds of people that it is acceptable because it is on the news, the TV, all over the place. Many men in churches have their wives waking up in the middle of the night to find that they are not in bed with them but are downstairs watching pornography. They are not able to have a proper sex life with their wives because they are feeding on filth. It is not necessarily their hearts that have the issue but it is down to the lust of the eyes which is feeding the flesh and not feeding them spiritually.

Ultimately, it is not fulfilling but just fleeting moments of euphoria and excitement and adrenalin rush. Sadly, it has been put out there for so long across many platforms that if you are not in it, you are not normal. What the enemy does with guys especially Christian fellas, is that he will provide the temptation to look at stuff, they give in to the temptation and look at it and that is the triple whammy, 'the thought, the temptation and the guilt'. They end up feeling so guilty, filthy and trapped for doing it again; thinking 'oh my God it's got me in dark doing secret things and I can't talk to, my leaders, friends or anyone about it'. These guys get so bound up in this stuff and the enemy convinces them that they are the only ones doing it. It paralyses men in the church because of guilt, they are afraid to cry out for help. But as soon as the men start to confess, speak and talk about it there is freedom. When this comes out in the light, the person feels free and has people who are willing to support with prayer around him.

The enemy uses the guilt of carrying something deplorable (something you feel if someone knows about would be shameful), to destroy marriages, families and self. The heaviness of carrying something and thinking 'what would people say' if they knew their dad, uncle, brother or leader was involved in something so shameful is unbearable. They often think 'will they push me aside, divorce me' etc.? These are the thoughts the devil puts in people's minds.

However, calling on the name of Jesus is the only way out; calling on the name that is above every other name, the greatest name- Jesus. Simply saying 'Jesus help me, I am caught and I am looking at things help me and wash me in your blood'. There have been so many men's meetings where a man has got up to confess his addiction to pornography and instead of the shock horror that he expects to get in response to the confession, other men have gone and embraced him and said that they had either been victims before or close to becoming victims too.

Unfortunately, pornography is all in our face these days; people are born into a world where gender change is going on so it seems natural. Over the years, the media has promoted this stuff. The Bible tells us that it is detestable to God for a man to dress up as a woman and vice versa; there are no blurred lines, and it can't be dressed up. But in today's society it is okay to be what you want when you want, so one day you can be Billy and the next day Milly and the world

70

would embrace you. The more bizarre people become the more they will get accepted. If you have any opposing view to accepting these absurdities you are in trouble. If a family were to sit together at a certain time of night to watch TV, they would all be watching porn, not necessarily the worst kind but, the subtle type. On that TV screen, every thought that had ever popped up in the mind flashes before you because of what you see on the screen. The second look at a girl passing on the street, the fighting, anger, foul language, all of that stuff is on the screen in just one day, even in half an hour. Indeed all have sinned and fallen short of God's glory.

We are pressed on every side of the globe with pornography. You can't get away from it everywhere you go. The media uses it to sell things and the enemy uses the guilt from looking at porn to keep us down. When you start speaking about the lust of the flesh, the lust of the eyes, the pride of life or the pull of the flesh, you have freedom and you are free from it. But if you don't talk about it because the enemy tells you that you are the only one engaged in that, looking at that, the only one with the dodgy eyes, **you** … the preacher, the man, the brother, then condemnation sets in.

At the one-day Bold Encounter meetings, men who confess their pornography sins feel so relieved once it is out there because a yoke is taken off them because it has been brought into the light. *James 5:16 says "confess your sins to one another so that you may be healed"*, there is healing in that confession; there is healing.

This stuff is addictive

The question remains, why are people addicted to that stuff? It is because it is feeding the flesh. The devil imitates the intimacy that God planned for a man and his wife and offers a false intimacy through the screen and a false intimacy through a wrongful relationship. It is all fleeting. Sexual sin is the only sin that is from the inside, so when 2 people have sex, they leave little pieces of each other with the person they have been intimate with. The stuff that no one else sees is left behind. When you get on the wrong side of that you are driven into a closet by the guilt and fear of what the world would say. People seem more worried about what the world would say than what Jesus would say. This is because in the church there is a judgemental attitude, so people cannot admit to this stuff. The attitude is "you can't be saved and be a part of this church and be looking at that stuff, Jesus is not with you". The church pretends the issue of pornography does not exist within its four walls. But what goes on behind closed doors is unbelievable.

In the Old Testament, God told them, you are going into the land of the Canaanites who have false gods, are having sex in the temples and prostituting themselves all over the place, so whatever you do, don't do that. But the Israelites got caught in the same things and were copying what the Canaanites were doing. The only way you can copy what a nation is doing is because of the fleshy desire. The feeling of 'oh my gosh what is that? what is going on there?' takes over and then the culture of alcohol, recreational drugs becomes normal. When you get influenced by that all your inhibitions go away and you can be who you want to be and do whatever you like. The enemy uses nightclubs, drugs, darkness and everything. God told the Israelites not to copy but throughout history, we find that humanity is continually copying humanity. This is happening because the enemy has taken us down and keeps doing it. He wants to kill, steal and destroy; he wants to destroy the human family unit.

If you are involved in this stuff, the best way to come to terms and deal with it is to talk about it. Get someone you can trust, you do not need more than one or 2 people. And if you are a married man your prayer should be 'Lord give me eyes only for my wife'. *Isaiah 50:7 says "For the Lord GOD will help me; therefore shall I not be confounded: therefore have I set my face like a flint, and I know that I shall not be ashamed".* Jesus set His face like a flint to the cross. He is the one we should be copying and following. It all comes back to the cross and Jesus. This is not going to go away with a one-time prayer, this is something that needs to be worked at, and you have to press in, resist it with blood, sweat and tears. There is an old saying "sex thrives on rock and roll", which is so real. The lifestyle of sex drugs and rock and roll is a lying lifestyle that ends up in a dead-end for your life. Your marriage is on the rocks, you can't have an intimate loving relationship with your wife, your kids are all over the place and you are carrying guilt, you feel sick to your stomach and your priorities are all over the place. What the enemy puts out there is all for the flesh, feeding the flesh because he knows our weaknesses.

Fight that sin and move it away

While doing one of his programs, sometime ago, Simon asked a man to ask the Holy Spirit to show him his secret sin. The man said, "I should confess lust but I like lust". You can't ask God to forgive you for something if you enjoy it and keep going back to it. You have to hate that sin and ask God to take it away from you; you have to deal with it. Fight it and move it away. That applies to everything e.g. lust, guilt, pride, greed whatever it is, because one thing may have grabbed hold of one person while another thing has someone else. Everyone has something that they are dealing with. Paul called it a thorn in the flesh that was left in there. Paul pleaded 3 times for God to take it away but God said "*my grace is sufficient for you*". God's grace, anointing, word and power are what it takes. It might take a lifetime to deal with this battle but you must stay strong and surrender yourself and hand the battle to the Lord because the battle belongs to God. Just because you are born again does not mean that you will have all of these battles taken away from you automatically, because it is an outside oppression from the eyes which can be bred from the inside. You may have to walk through Psalm 23 for the rest of your life and it might be with you till the day Jesus comes but you have to turn your back to this sin. It is not easy; none of this stuff is easy.

The love of money brings satisfaction to the flesh, 'I want to get another car, hang on a minute, I want another one'. The lies that the enemy shows is that when you get more of the fleshy things you will be satisfied with the nice car, watch, or TV. Then you get it, but the gratification is just for a short while; it is only a fleeting satisfaction and you are on to the next thing. If you do not have Jesus and Jesus is not living in you, you are looking for self-gratification and happiness outside with money and material things. You think these will bring you happiness but materialism and the love of money open the gateway to everything else.

When Simon decided to follow Christ 3 things left him; *lust for money, love of drink, and swearing*. But he still struggled with looking at pretty girls and he had to keep himself on the straight and narrow continuously asking God to give him eyes only for his wife. He still struggles with anger and the struggle with road rage is getting better, but that's the journey of life. There is no perfect man alive, we all fall short daily; "*all have fallen short of the glory of God*". Each day we fall short in thought word or deed.

Set your face like a flint

In following Christ it does not mean all the struggles will end. In following Christ it is clear that we are on our way to heaven but in this journey of life there will be troubles, hardship, fears, tears, addiction, joy, etc. that is life. It is learning to deal with what is right and wrong that matters. The sad thing is that the world believes that freedom is only gained by doing everything and anything as they want. The reality, however, is that this leads to bondage and addictions. We have to live by rules and the freedom is by living with Jesus. In Christ is the freedom, through obedience and submission to Christ. There is total freedom in Christ. That should be the heartbeat of our lives, it should be a 24/7 thing, all day long not just a Sunday morning thing. There should be no day off from saying 'help me, Lord, I've got a difficult day today, going through certain areas of life'. The enemy does not take a holiday; he does not jump on Easy Jet and say 'I am off guys; I am going to leave you for a while'. If you are sold out to Christ are you willing to pay the price? Christ has redeemed us from hell thank God Christ has paid the ultimate price for us but we have to deal with our earthly emotions and body.

We all want to believe that we are holy and there is nothing wrong with us in our lives but even someone who is sold out to Jesus, who is not sold out to church but has decided to follow Jesus, is still subject to temptations. When you start to follow Jesus you will get daily convictions by the power of the Holy Spirit because of what the world is bringing to you and not because of what you want to do. Even as you walk through the 'valley of Bluewater' to do your shopping or go to work, there are posters all over the place and things happening around that bring about heavy oppression. You can't escape unless you stay in your house and throw your gadgets out and keep yourself free from all that. However, as soon as you step out, everything is thrown back in your face. That is why getting into the scripture and knowing your Bible is important. The Bible tells us that *"the weapons of our warfare are not carnal they are mighty through God to the pulling down of strongholds"*. If you had a struggle with lust, greed or pornography, it is a stronghold that the enemy has built in you and you can't bring it down instantly. Sometimes, you have to break it down brick by brick, that is why the Bible says we have to take these thoughts captive and hand them to Jesus because we can't handle them on our own. It is the thought that is the problem and not just the act. The action is already done in the head before it manifests and that is frightening. But you can choose what to think. Things will come into your head but you can decide whether to sit down and have a cup of tea with that thought or just dismiss it. The battlefield is in the mind. We are all in church, looking nice, holding hands and being holy and no one sees our thoughts but Jesus. No one can see inside our brains, we can act like Christians, and do not go down the road of the physical act, but it can all still be happening in our heads. It says in the book of Revelations that the devil is the accuser of the brethren. He is spending day and night time running back and forth saying to God 'did you see what Ben was thinking in his head', etc. If we keep a short account of the wrong thoughts and we confess it to God, then all God sees is not these wrong thoughts in Ben's head but his son Jesus. He just sees him cleansed by the blood of Jesus. But if we hang on to that stuff, God will look down and say, yes I see it, he is getting himself involved in that stuff and I can't do anything about it because sin separates me from him. This happens because we are the ones hanging onto that stuff-it comes down to choice.

When we think of the mind, the power of the mind and the brain, what drives that is what the eyes see. So if you live in a culture that thrives on sex, drugs and rock and roll your eyes will engage and tell you how your flesh should live. The Bible tells us the eyes are the windows of the soul. So if you are going around the shops and all you see is stuff that is sexualised, that is a driver. If you listen to advertising that says you can have a soda, it is not going to cost you anything you start to think 'hang on a minute I can adopt that' and the greed sets in. The battle of the mind is the biggest battle that anyone would have. Wherever you are in life or in ministry or whoever you are you might look like the greatest teacher and preacher and seem like you have it all together behind the pulpit and colleges but no one sees your mind. You might look good and sound good on the outside but you might have things spinning around in your mind that need to be dealt with. So the only way to deal with these thoughts is to call on the greatest name Jesus. Because if you let these thoughts fester, all of a sudden the next time you are making love to your wife you may be seeing the little girl down the road who smiled at you or the stuff that you saw on your television. Your mind is overtaken by everything the eye sees. Our culture is driven by sight and instant gratification.

The financial implications of this instant gratification, the 'buy, buy' now syndrome is huge and there is so much public debt. There is the constant desire for money; money makes people want to do anything for it because the world has said that money will open up the gateway to everything but what does it open up to? Often it is sex, drugs and rock and roll.

Simon's son applied for a loan a while ago and within less than 5 minutes, the money was in his account just like that without walking out of his front door, just after click-click; that click culture is an issue.

Many people have several Amazon boxes in their homes of stuff they bought just after one click; they are buying all sorts of things. And the delivery man is going 'oh no, not that Ben's house again'! It is instant; it comes the next day to your house you don't have to move from your house.

Even now with the advancement of technology, people can speak to their devices and get things done. The power of speech is dangerous, what you can do with the power of speech is so dangerous and you can get trapped into online gambling, porn, shopping and the most addictive thing out there is gambling. As pornography is destructive for the family, so is gambling. And the issue is with the 'hope'; the hope that next time there will be a big win. A guy lost his business, house, everything because of a scratch card because he kept hoping that the next one would be the big one. A pound here, a tenner there etc. all adds up. You go to the corner shop and you see a single mother who can barely survive buying scratch cards. The whole world is scratching in more ways than one; everyone is scratching an itch that can't be fulfilled. Gambling is the worst, the world of the lottery is so addictive, and it is everywhere. Funnily the Christian will say if I win a million the tithe is going to be good, God if you just let me win this, I'm going to drop some money in church.

You can walk into your local Asda at 10 in the morning and hear people talking about popping onto the betting shop to place a bet on a horse or something. Or they just bet on their phones. The issue like we mentioned earlier is with the access, easy access to everything. It even goes as far as bingo. It is all made to look like fun, it's addictive and pulls you in so much that some people rather than spend money on food for their kids are spending it on gambling on the scratch card. Some are also trying to beat the system using credit cards to gamble because it does not feel like real money and they end up in multiple debts that they can't even pay off because the big win they are after never happens.

There is one answer to all this stuff and his name is Jesus. *"If the Son therefore shall make you free, ye shall be free indeed"* (John 8: 36 KJV). It is impossible to get away from all the stuff mentioned above because of the accessibility. No matter how much you are in the world, when you come away from your study or out and about it is dangled in your face and everything is just there. We all need to be very careful, that is why guys need to make sure they have time and space alone with God. Get on your face and your knees before God and be very protective of that time with God. Just talk to God, he sees in your mind and though God knows everything we still need to speak to him. We need to verbalise all that is on our minds before God. It is like having a child, you want your child to come to you and tell you what he/she needs or what he/she has done wrong and say 'I'm sorry dad I have hurt you'. And then you can embrace your child and forgive that child and say in return 'don't do that again, it's okay'. That's what the Father wants from us and that is the power of the blood through his son Jesus.

You can have all the right people and doctors around you to discuss your addictions etc. but until you confess all to Jesus you will still be trapped. Sometimes we have to get to the root of all the addictions and the only way to do that is through the conviction of the Holy Spirit. You can spend thousands and months going to see one Psychiatrist, Therapist or the other and get no solution. But you can spend just a few minutes with the Holy Spirit and cut to the core of the issue in minutes.

A while ago Simon was with a good friend a Christian who in his 50's was driven by fear. Fear and doubt are huge tools of the enemy. They asked the

Holy Spirit to reveal the root of the fear. The man then remembered that when he was 8 years old on a school bus, the driver got off the bus and he was frightened the driver would not get back and that he would not get home. That was the door that the enemy used to come into his life and from that day, he lived in fear, there was a stronghold of fear built up. Once the Holy Spirit revealed that to him, he was able to work on that fear. That's what we have got in our armoury as Christian men and women. God is known as the almighty counsellor, He is our guide, counsellor and king and there is nothing new under the sun that He does not know about. We can spend thousands of pounds sitting and listening to doctor, lawyer, counsellors etc. and it will help to a degree but it will not bring freedom because these issues are spiritual so we need to come to God. He is the greatest life coach anyone could ever have and it is free and he frees us.

When we say who the Son sets free is free indeed, it means spiritually we are free but then, the battles begin and because we now have the Holy Spirit, He convicts us of things we used to do before that are not right, so the old man should be crucified, buried and gone. But what people do is that they do not fully bury the old man but carry him on their backs and all of a sudden get into a situation and rather than put their trust in Jesus, they get the old man out again and say old man deal with that. The old man should be gone; we have to be born again, John 3:3 and 2 Corinthians 5: 17 say we have to be *'changed'*. That is a process and a journey, *"yea though I walk through the valley"*. Life is a journey so following Christ as a real man for Christ is a narrow path and not a Vegas path. It is a path that is thin, a tight rope not a great big wide bridge that is lit up to guide to the other side; it is a walk of faith; *"The just shall live by faith"*, we do not live by sight, we live in this dark world by faith. The parable of the sower comes to mind here, so when the word goes out it lands on 4 soils therefore, only a quarter of the people who hear the word would accept it. That road is narrow, only a quarter of the ground is fertile.

How does one then increase his faith, It comes from hearing a message from the word of God. Consequently, if a man is addicted to pornography the way to get out of it is by confessing the sin, speaking and talking and just being open and honest and coming to the word, reading the word; it is a process. The battle belongs to the Lord is a great scripture but you still have to live, you cannot sit on your backside and do nothing. You have to take steps and move forward. And you do it with the Lord and the word of God. It all comes back to the cross because it is the answer to everything. The cross is like a hub and is like a wheel with the spooks of life coming off it but it all comes back to the centre- the word of God and Jesus. So set your face like a flint towards the cross. You can only do it through Jesus, through submission and obedience, total submission; bend your knees to Jesus. His name is the greatest name in heaven and earth.

Forgotten Men of Church

The biggest challenge a man in the world of the church faces today, is being forgotten. Sadly there are men who have been forgotten in the church, men of strong faith.

When a man rises in faith and has a real calling on his life, it is a threat to the leader of the church. Men of strong faith intimidate the leaders of churches and some of these leaders should probably not be leading the church. If you have been brought up in the church you know no different. There are men out there who are seeking Jesus and when they go to the local church and step in the door they see what is happening, the flag-waving and all that, they just turn around thinking that it is all weird.

Pastor Ben recalls that when he left school, he went into bricklaying. This was a real man's world and he loved it. He knew Christ a little bit and for about 10 years all he did was work in bricklaying gangs all over the place and this got him in a lot of trouble. But thanks to God, he was set free from that, so when he remembers his bricklaying colleagues, he knows for a fact that they would not step into a church; and that is sad. They would be like 'why would I come into the church to be told by the leader that I am not worthy? I already know I'm not worthy; all I want is a bit of love. All I want is someone to tell me that everything will be okay'.

Unfortunately, religion does not do that instead it makes up a false environment. These men, Scaffolders, Lorry drivers, Truckers etc. big tough men in an environment that is a 'Hard Hat'area, real cavemen, are not seen in the church. Simon has a mate who had to form something called 'Men in Sheds' in Ipswich because there were no programs for men in his church. He holds a meeting once a month in a Portakabin with fish and chips. One night while speaking in one of the units on the farm during a gospel challenge a guy responded to the challenge but soon after doing that he was accosted by some other men from the local church inviting him to attend their church meetings etc. the man ran away and never came back.

The focus of Real Men for Christ, a program Simon is involved in, is leading other men to Christ and following the **Real Man** Jesus because with men you have to walk with them and they have to see things for themselves. The church however does not seem to walk with them but pushes them aside many times because the church does not to know what to do with them. There is a certain robotic man that the church will adopt because a real man is frightening to reverend, pastor or vicar because he will let you have it as it is. This does not mean that every man in the church is not a real man but that sometimes men can't be men. Men can't literarily say how they feel or express themselves for many reasons. And when you look at men's ministries in the church it is pretty lame and weak. There are great men in church but they are getting burnt out. A lot of these men's ministries or Saturday breakfast or evening curry meetings are nothing more than clubs.

On a trip to Valencia for a men's meeting a while ago, 50 to 100 expatriates came together. After the talk given by Simon challenging them to be kingdom men and to have a go for Jesus, the organiser got up and said "that was nice blokes, see you again next year". There is nothing wrong with that, but what is missing is talking about the blood of Jesus, and sins being forgiven, what men have done in the past, the gangs, the drinking, violence, womanising, pornography and all the stuff in the world that men can get caught up in. This does not get addressed. The church does not talk about the real issues that men go through. What happens is that men become Sunday morning warriors. How many of the men in church today with their hands raised can be a disciple?

While in the police Simon was part of a team, with men he could rely on, in riots and tough situations, shoulder to shoulder, fighting for each other. It is like the story in the new testament where 4 men grab hold of the four corners of their friend's mat and carry him to see Jesus and when they see that they can't get to Jesus, they tear the roof of someone's house to get him to Jesus. Men need other men around them that will carry them. The pandemic has exploded the doors off the churches and has exposed that the church is very thin spiritually. This is why men have been pushed out of churches because they can't be real but puppets.

During one of the Bold Encounters an event organised to bring guys together to talk about their stuff, one guy said that there was no one in his church that he could rely on. He said the men were too frightened to talk about their issues openly because of the rejection that they could face if they got up and admitted they have a problem. So they are living this life on the surface but inside, they are broken, this is not what Jesus wants. He said *"come to me all you who are weary and heavy-laden and I will give you rest"* but the system of the church does not allow men to get to Jesus. It is like the Pharisees, Sadducees and the crowd around Jesus. Like with the woman with the issue of blood, the religious crowd is stopping real men from getting to Jesus and men are frightened to say it as it is.

If you put men in the right environment that is safe they will talk. There are so many issues out there for men; one of the biggest is the relationship with their earthly fathers and Words said over them, especially words said by their earthly fathers. There are guys in their 60's and 70's who have never told their children that they love them because of what has happened to them, generational issues. These are men in the church who will say my children know I love them, but that is not the case- the men need to say it to their children. When you get men to open up they get a feeling of being alright and okay. They realise that to a degree every Tom, Dick and Harry is in a similar boat and they feel like they are normal. They feel so relieved that the guy they see every Sunday with the wife and 2 kids who seems perfect also has issues that he is dealing with and is also broken on the inside. When the Holy Spirit gets them to open up, they realise that all men have struggles and issues. When they start to talk about these issues and un-pack them they feel better.

Men have carried all these struggles for so long because the devil has told them that if they reveal to anyone that they like to drink, smoke or go to the club, or look at things, that they will be pushed out of the church and never allowed to return. The enemy's biggest lie is that you are on your own, he wants to separate, isolate and destroy, *"the thief comes to steal kill and destroy" (John 10:10).* He comes to steal peace and destroy men internally by constantly saying to them 'are you sure God said... are you sure if you tell the leader of the church that you have anger issues, are jealous, have wandering eyes or like a little drink at the weekend, or about the story of yourself that they will let you stay in this church? Just smile and pretend all is well'. There are so many broken men in the church, who look at their Pastor all put together in the leather jacket and skinny jeans, looking perfect, with the beautiful tan, lovely looking wife and kids praising the Lord, with amazing testimonies etc. and these men feel unable to approach the 'perfect' Pastor with their issues. This perfect image the pastor portrays is not real, and many people buy into that. Many times it is about showmanship, feelings and emotion, euphoria and adrenalin rush but it is not real. When people then get kicked up the backside by life as often happens they become frustrated because they did not bargain for that.

Men enter into spiritual warfare with themselves simply because they can't talk to the leadership. In many of the big churches, everything looks perfect from the coffee to the musicians but there is a lot of control from the leadership. So if you are a man who can see through the rubbish you will sit back and say "look at those idiots up there, I have come here with desperate needs, addiction, exhausted, emotionally tired and all I see is a production, I might as well go to the cinema. I need someone to help me and talk to me about how to address my sin. I am fed up of watching the show and hearing about how great you are, tell me about Jesus"

A mate of Simon's at a big church in London, who is a big fella and has a big voice that other men are attracted to, is not being used by his church in men's ministry, despite coming up with ideas and suggestions. As a result, he is now looking to move to another church because the church has not recognised his gift as a leader of men. If you have men in the church that other men are drawn to, that is the church. The Theological colleges and ministry schools and all the supernatural schools out there are not equipping men, it is all fluffy stuff. They are not addressing issues like being irritated at home, frustrated at work, road rage, guilt and bags of stuff hanging around men. You can also see on the faces of men the cry "help me; someone help me".

In the Real Man for Christ a ministry led by Simon, what they believe the Lord has given them is 4 pillars for men to stand on.

1. Identity

Where is your identity, what is your identity in, is it your house, car, wife, football, or is it in Christ. It has to be in Jesus Christ- "*Seek ye first the kingdom*". Where is the signpost of your life pointing? If it is pointing back to you or somewhere else that is idolatry, and you are in trouble. It has to be Jesus completely "*it is not I that lives but Christ lives in me*". It has to be surrender and obedience to Christ; that is where a man's identity has to be.

2. Authority.

If you know your identity in Christ and you believe the Bible is the word of God and not just a nice book full of stories, you know that you have been given the authority to go out and preach to all 4 corners of the earth, to heal the sick and to drive out demons. People always forget the portion about driving out demons but a lot of stuff that goes on in the church is demonic, pagan and occultism; it runs through in many churches.

3. Cost.

It costs something; if you join the army you don't say I will join if my conditions apply and you do not shoot at me. It is going to cost you time, your life. You are going into enemy territory you can be fired at, starved and tortured for Christ. Are you prepared to die for Jesus?

4. Discipleship and Discipline.

To be able to pay that cost, it can't be done alone. The Church is lacking a lot of real discipleship and pastoral care. According to Pastor Ben, he feels like during the Pandemic he failed miserably at being a Pastor. What the church tries to equip pastors with for pastoral care is not adequate. When a real crisis comes in, it is almost impossible to a degree because the Pastor starts to become inwardly focused and starts to look at things differently. If the Pastor does not get himself right, he can't pastor right. With Discipline and Discipleship, it is clear that we need each other. *Ecclesiastics 4:9 "says two are better than 1 and a 3 braided cord is not easily broken"*. We need each other; we need to walk with one another. How would you bring someone to the faith if you do not walk with them and you don't know how to walk with them?

We need to be disciplined but beyond that sometimes we need to get down in the dirt and get our faces looking towards the Lord and do it on our own. When David was in Ziklag he had to strengthen himself in the Lord his God (1st Samuel 30:6). It is funny that people will have your back when the going is good but as soon as something happens that smells a little bad, they turn on you. But that is not just in the Christian world but a general thing. When Simon was in the police force he got suspended, he knew hundreds of people who turned their backs on him. They would walk past him in the gym and ignore him, only a handful of fellas, stood by him. Many people have hundreds of followers on Facebook but when things go wrong for those people who will be there to pick them up and carry them to Jesus? When they are laid on the stretcher and it has gone wrong and they are exhausted who will say 'I will tear the roof down and get you to Jesus'.

How many men would stand by another when things go wrong? Who will lift their heads above the parapet? Where are the Joshua's and the Caleb's who will say, 'hang on we have seen everything but our God is able?' when the others say we AIN'T GOING. Where are the real men for Christ?

While Simon was on a ranch in Texas during a retreat, someone asked if he had seen the sunrise early, and as Simon walked out he saw the sun coming out and he felt he was on the Lord's shoulders and the Lord was pointing out men sticking up their hands. Before this, he had a similar experience while driving down the M25 where he heard God say to him 'real men for Christ where are they,' John Wesley said *"Give me one hundred preachers who fear nothing but sin, and desire nothing but God, and I care not a straw whether they be clergymen or laymen; such alone will shake the gates of hell and set up the kingdom of heaven on Earth."* Gideon did not need a big army but the world needs men who know their identity, their authority, are willing to pay the price and are ready to disciple other men. If there are little groups of them all over the country, little fires, it would make a big impact.

The Lord is not looking for national organisations; he can't work in that because they get in the way of the Holy Spirit because it is controlled. With big

97

organisational, systematic churches, it's often about 'me, me, me;' they look good, attractive to the human eye. Because there are a lot of people, it does not mean it is right, or that a revival is happening or the teaching is correct. Many churches pray "Lord rain down your revival on us" but the revival has to be personal. The revival starts with the individual, with repentance and stripping back of everything *"he is the gardener and I am the vinedresser"*. Pastor Ben prayed a few years ago that God would strip him back and he found that the striping back is painful but it is moulding him into the character that God wants him to be. He is no longer moulded by the systematic church or religion; he is learning that he belongs to Jesus and trying to live a holy life. We have people with spiritual gifts not living a spiritual life, thank God for the scripture that says *"all have sinned and fall short of the glory of God"* because it helps to keep one's head above water. According to Pastor, Ben sometimes it feels like he is drowning in his mess, motivational speakers, Ted talkers, church, religion, pulpit rubbish. The church is drowning him because it is not giving him the truth but flooding him with jargon and clichés and Ted talks, with things that are stifling and not helping him grow. Sometimes it is difficult to even shout out Jesus, in Church.

What is your focus as a Christian?

A couple of years ago Simon was in a group of churches together in Luton and he asked them 2 questions which he commonly asks groups that he meets with. The first question was "what is the most important thing as a Christian in your life?" They came up with lots of varied answers, so Simon asked about their relationship with Jesus and they answered "we never thought about that". You can be busy doing this and that; the church will keep you busy, sometimes even doing the devils work, and not the work of the kingdom. Matt 7: 22 describes it clearly *"Many will say to me on that day, 'Lord, Lord, did we not prophesy in your name and in your name drive out demons and in your name perform many miracles?"*- 'Lord I was in the church doing this and that for you' but Christ will say 'where was your love for me, where was your true sacrifice where were you trying to seek me? Where was your heart? Go from me I never knew you.' When we look at David, he had his good and bad sides, he made loads of mistakes but his heart was with God and that was what God loved about him. His heart was after God but he still had wandering eyes and had a man killed because he wanted the man's wife. So what we have to understand is that although we have a heart for Jesus we must also live for Jesus, in this sinful world. We have to follow Jesus. We have to come to the cross every morning and go through the cross and die to self *"I have been crucified with Christ and I no longer live, but Christ lives in me"* (Galatians 2: 20). Dying to self is not coming across the pulpits in England these days.

The second question that Simon asked is what is the most exciting thing you can do as a Christian? Again the answers were varied and Simon said 'how about being part of the process that brings someone to faith?' and many answered 'what's that?'. Many have a different concept of what church is but there is nothing greater than being part of the process which brings someone to the faith. There is nothing greater than seeing someone snatched from the gates of hell. Everything changes when someone is led to Christ. It is more exciting than putting on Lycra and riding a bike or climbing a mountain or even jumping out off an aircraft. To see someone give their life to Jesus is exciting, like the thief on the cross who at the last minute turned to Jesus and asked Him to remember him, Jesus knew the thief's heart.

Let salvation be the focus

Pastor Ben has had experiences of people who have lived their lives away from Church and Christ and in the last breath have accepted Jesus. Some of these people have said that the church hurt and abused them and some have said they were pushed away by the church. Unfortunately, the church is trying to build 'a church' and it is not focusing on pulling people out of hell. A lot of people have been away from the church because of the church. But it is not the 'church' but the people in the church that abuse others. With the pandemic, the Lord is stripping back stuff. But the stories of people in the hospice and the look on their faces when they give their lives to Jesus can't be compared to anything. When someone is staring down the lens of death what happens next? Knowing that Jesus loves them brings hope. You can't get that anywhere else; no pagan minister can give such hope. The only hope that one will find is hope in Christ, through Christ, in the word of God. There is nothing more powerful than seeing someone coming to Christ maybe at the last moments of their life, like the thief on the cross with their last few breaths. There are so many stories of people who are dealing with stuff that they have bottled up and carried all their life and at the last

101

breath they let those things go and accept Jesus and are snatched into the kingdom. There is nothing more powerful.

Sadly the church has become more business-oriented rather than salvation minded; the church is more corporate and has lost the spiritual punch. Why are people in the church today? It is not to give their wages but to get their lives right, repent, be covered in the blood of Jesus and walk out of the church knowing their redeemer lives. There's the deal. In a lot of these churches they say that you are saved when you just accept Jesus, there is no mention of repentance, sin, or coming to the cross; it is just accepting Jesus and you are okay. That is the lie that is being told to people. When you accept Christ repentance is needed. Repentance is needed daily, morning, afternoon, night, on the road, when travelling etc. We need to repent from, anger, guilt, etc. asking the Lord to forgive us and wash us in the blood.

When we have a bit of anger or lust etc., the enemy will run to the Lord to say have you seen that? Have you seen what Ben did? And if you have not confessed that to Jesus the devil can capitalise on that but if you have already confessed it, the Lord will say, "I see my son Jesus on Ben, he knows his failings and he is dealing with it, it is not hidden." That is why we must keep short accounts and continuously repent.

"*The wages of Sin is death but the gift of God is eternal life*" (Romans 6: 23). This is the truth. If you know the truth, it will set you free.

Last Word

If anything in this book has led you to make Jesus Christ the Lord of your life, then say this simple prayer, wherever you are:

Heavenly Father please forgive me for the sin, the wrong stuff in my life. I turn my back on that stuff now, and repent of all the sin, and I accept Jesus Christ into my life to be my Lord and Saviour from this day forward. Amen

If anyone would like a `Free` Bible from #Christian Straight Talk – the please email the guys at

Simon@christianstraighttalk.uk